500 Things
Your Sunday School
Teacher Tried To Tell You

500 Things
Your Sunday School
Teacher Tried To Tell You

...But you were too busy
playing with the flannelgraph
of Moses in the bulrushes
to listen.

Written and Compiled by
ARLEN PRICE

Star Song Publishing Group
     a division of Jubilee Communications, Inc.
P.O. Box 150009
Nashville, Tennessee 37215

ISBN # 1-56233-038-1

Printed in the United States of America
First Printing, August 1992

              2 3 4 5 6 7 8 9 — 97 96 95 94 93

To Jeanie,

The most important thing you've taught me that I didn't learn in Sunday school is that a great wife is more valuable than precious jewels (from Proverbs 31:10).

Praise God, from whom all blessings flow; Praise him, all creatures here below; Praise him above, ye heav'nly host; Praise Father, Son, and Holy Ghost.

"Praise God from Whom All Blessings Flow"
Thomas Ken, 1695

Library paste, despite being a taste sensation, has absolutely no nutritional value whatsoever.

Man does not live on bread alone, but on every word that comes from the mouth of God.

Matthew 4:4

Things Your Sunday School Teacher Told You...

Intelligence is not measured by aptitude tests or material success but by the depths of one's reverence for the Lord (from Proverbs 1:7).

The law of the Lord is a friend in both fair and foul weather (from Psalm 1).

Marry into a family that will enable your children to feel proud of both sides of the house.

—Robert E. Lee

In the beginning God created the heavens and the earth.

Genesis 1:1

But You Were Too Busy to Listen

If Adam taught Sunday school his lesson would be:
You cannot fulfill God's plan for your life alone.

Lessons from The Sermon on the Mount
The fifth chapter of Matthew

Blessed are the poor in spirit, for theirs is the
kingdom of heaven.

Verse 3

Blessed are those who mourn, for they will be
comforted.

Verse 4

Blessed are the meek, for they will inherit the earth.

Verse 5

Blessed are those who hunger and thirst for righteousness, for they will be filled.

Verse 6

Blessed are the merciful, for they will be shown mercy.

Verse 7

Blessed are the pure in heart, for they will see God.

Verse 8

But You Were Too Busy to Listen

Blessed are the peacemakers, for they will be called sons of God.

Verse 9

Blessed are those who are persecuted because of righteousness, for theirs is the kingdom of heaven.

Verse 10

Blessed are you when people insult you, persecute you and falsely say all kinds of evil against you because of me . . . because great is your reward in heaven, for in the same way they persecuted the prophets who were before you.

Verses 11–12

 13

Things Your Sunday School Teacher Told You...

Of a surety at the Day of Judgment it will be demanded of us, not what we have read, but what we have done; not how well we have spoken, but how holily we have lived.

—Thomas a´ Kempis

The best teachers a child will ever have answer to the names "Mom" and "Dad" (from Proverbs 1:8–9).

God responds to our anger against him with anger against us (from Psalm 2:1–6).

Love your enemies and pray for those who persecute you.

Matthew 5:44

But You Were Too Busy to Listen

Blessed assurance, Jesus is mine! Oh, what a foretaste of glory divine!

"Blessed Assurance, Jesus Is Mine"
Fanny J. Crosby, 1873

Life can only be understood backwards; but it must be lived forwards.

—Soren Kierkegaard

God created man in his own image, in the image of God he created him; male and female he created them.

Genesis 1:27

If Eve taught Sunday school her lesson would be: Temptation yields bitter fruit.

If you forgive men when they sin against you, your heavenly Father will also forgive you.

Matthew 6:14

If you do not forgive men their sins, your Father will not forgive your sins.

Matthew 6:15

There is an eternity behind and an eternity before, and this little speck in the center, however long, is comparatively but a minute.

—John Brown

But You Were Too Busy to Listen

The only certain future for those who associate with dishonest, sinful people is no future at all (from Proverbs 1:10–19).

The love that shines from God's face will illuminate the darkest moments of your life (from Psalm 4:6–8).

Where your treasure is, there your heart will be also.

Matthew 6:21

Things Your Sunday School Teacher Told You...

Immortal Love, forever full, Forever flowing free,
Forever shared, forever whole, A never ebbing sea!
"Immortal Love, Forever Full"
John Greenleaf Whittier, 1866

Begin to be now what you will be hereafter.
—St. Jerome

The LORD will fight for you; you need only to be
still.

Exodus 14:14

If Abel taught Sunday school his lesson would be:
God will honor our righteousness with justice.

 18

But You Were Too Busy to Listen

O̲ur Lord has written the promise of the resurrection, not in books alone, but in every leaf in springtime.

—Martin Luther

T̲he only premium you ever have to pay for the best and most secure insurance policy in the world is to maintain a pure and faithful heart (from Proverbs 2:7–8).

T̲here are those who think that standing tall and proud is a virtue—but God isn't one of them (from Psalm 5:5).

Things Your Sunday School Teacher Told You...

Jesus loves me! this I know, for the Bible tells me so; Little ones to him belong; They are weak, but he is strong.

> "Jesus Loves Me"
> Anna B. Warner, 1860

In all my perplexities and distresses, the Bible has never failed to give me light and strength.

> —Robert E. Lee

Honor your father and your mother.

> Exodus 20:12

Things Your Sunday School Teacher Told You...

If Noah taught Sunday school his lesson would be: Obedience to God is more important than winning friends and influencing people.

The harvest is plentiful but the workers are few.

Matthew 9:37

He who dwelleth in peace is suspicious of none, but he who is discontented and restless is tossed with many suspicions, and is neither quiet himself nor suffereth others to be quiet.

—Thomas a´ Kempis

But You Were Too Busy to Listen

A loving and faithful attitude is a finer adornment in the eyes of God than precious jewels (from Proverbs 3:3–4).

A physician may be able to heal your body but only God can heal your soul (from Psalm 6:2–4).

What goes into a man's mouth does not make him "unclean," but what comes out of his mouth, that is what makes him "unclean."

Matthew 15:11

Things Your Sunday School Teacher Told You...

My hope is built on nothing less, Than Jesus' blood and righteousness; I dare not trust the sweetest frame, But wholly lean on Jesus' name.

"The Solid Rock" Edward Mote, 1832

Nothing can make a man truly great but being truly good.

—Matthew Henry

Be holy because I, the LORD your God, am holy.

Leviticus 19:2

If Abraham taught Sunday school his lesson would be: Your blessings will outnumber the stars if your life shines with faithfulness to God.

But You Were Too Busy to Listen

If you have faith as small as a mustard seed, you can say to this mountain, "Move from here to there" and it will move. Nothing will be impossible for you.

Matthew 17:20

To do it no more is the truest repentance.

—Martin Luther

Honoring the Lord is what really makes a person healthy, wealthy, and wise (from Proverbs 3:7–10).

The arms of the Lord are a shelter from the storms of life (from Psalm 7:1–2).

Things Your Sunday School Teacher Told You...

I tell you the truth, unless you change and become like little children, you will never enter the kingdom of heaven.

Matthew 18:3

Though Satan should buffet, tho trials should come, Let this blest assurance control, That Christ has regarded my helpless estate, And hath shed his own blood for my soul.

"It Is Well with My Soul"
Horatio G. Spafford, 1873

Learn to say "No"; it will be of more use to you than to be able to read Latin.

—Charles Haddon Spurgeon

But You Were Too Busy to Listen

The LORD is slow to anger, abounding in love and forgiving sin and rebellion. Yet he does not leave the guilty unpunished.

Numbers 14:18

If Lot taught Sunday school his lesson would be: The pleasures of this world are as lasting as a puff of smoke.

It is easier for a camel to go through the eye of a needle than for a rich man to enter the kingdom of God.

Matthew 19:24

Things Your Sunday School Teacher Told You...

Absence of occupation is not rest.

—William Cowper

Just like a good parent, the Lord disciplines those he loves (from Proverbs 3:11–12).

The only leader who will never be impeached because of dishonesty and unfairness is the One who rules the universe (from Psalm 9:7–8).

The Sabbath was made for man, not man for the Sabbath.

Mark 2:27

But You Were Too Busy to Listen

There are heights of joy that I may not reach, Till I rest in peace with thee.

> "I Am Thine, O Lord"
> Fanny J. Crosby, 1875

He that falls into sin is a man; that grieves at it, is a saint; that boasteth of it is a devil.

> —Thomas Fuller

Know then in your heart that as a man disciplines his son, so the LORD your God disciplines you.

> Deuteronomy 8:5

If Sarah taught Sunday school her lesson would be: Patience is a virtue.

If anyone wants to be first, he must be the very last, and the servant of all.

Mark 9:35

Love is not one of the attributes of God, but the sum of them all.

—Reverend J. M. Gibbon

Wisdom is far easier to obtain—and much more valuable—than silver or gold (from proverbs 3:13–15).

"Two plus two equals five" is rare genius compared to the statement "There is no God" (from Psalm 14:1).

But You Were Too Busy to Listen

All things are possible with God.

Mark 10:27

There is a place of full release, Near to the heart of God, A place where all is joy and peace, Near to the heart of God.

"Near to the Heart of God"
Cleland B. McAfee, 1901

Hypocrisy—the only evil that walks invisible, except to God.

—John Milton

Things Your Sunday School Teacher Told You...

To the LORD your God belong the heavens, even the highest heavens, the earth and everything in it.

Deuteronomy 10:14

If Isaac taught Sunday school his lesson would be: A promise from God can be fulfilled through your life.

If you hold anything against anyone, forgive him, so that your Father in heaven may forgive you your sins.

Mark 11:25

But You Were Too Busy to Listen

Hope for the best, get ready for the worst, and then take what God chooses to send.

—Matthew Henry

Wise decisions make very soft pillows (from Proverbs 3:21–26).

There are a few key rules to keep in mind if you want to live in God's house:

Don't walk in the door unless your feet have been wiped clean of unrighteousness . . .

Tell the truth (and not just when it's sort of convenient) . . .

Love your neighbor (and that means all of them) . .

But You Were Too Busy to Listen

Turn away from those who are wicked (even if
   they seem to be having a lot of fun) . . .
Turn toward those who are good (even if they
   seem kind of boring) . . .
Keep your promises (even when you think that
   promise has been forgotten) . . .
Lend money without asking for it back (and
   don't charge interest in the meantime)
   (from Psalm 15).

Love the Lord your God with all your heart and
with all your soul and with all your mind and with
all your strength.

Mark 12:30

We walk by faith and not by sight.
>"We Walk by Faith and Not by Sight"
>Henry Alford, 1844

The greatest pleasure of life is love.
>—Sir William Temple

Be very careful to love the LORD your God.
>Joshua 23:11

If Jacob taught Sunday school his lesson would be:
All of God's children have a birthright to his
kingdom.

But You Were Too Busy to Listen

Watch and pray so that you will not fall into
temptation. The spirit is willing, but the body is
weak.

Mark 14:38

Be careful or you may be full of cares.
—Charles Haddon Spurgeon

If you're facing a person with a need, give them more
than a view of your back (from Proverbs 3:27–28).

You are the apple of God's eye (from Psalm 17:8).

Things Your Sunday School Teacher Told You...

G o into all the world and preach the good news to all creation.

Mark 16:15

O Jesus, thou hast promised, To all who follow thee, That where thou art in glory, There shall thy servant be.

"O Jesus, I Have Promised"
John E. Bode, 1868

T hose who are bound for heaven must be willing to swim against the stream.

—Matthew Henry

But You Were Too Busy to Listen

It is not by strength that one prevails; those who oppose the LORD will be shattered.

1 Samuel 2:9–10

If Rachel taught Sunday school her lesson would be: Share a drink from the well of living water.

Do to others as you would have them do to you.

Luke 6:31

A gold attendance star says you cared enough to give God your very best.

Christ is not valued at all unless He be valued above all.

—Augustine

The last thing your neighbor needs to worry about is you (from Proverbs 3:29–30).

God weighs our faithfulness toward him against his continual faithfulness toward us (from Psalm 18:25–26).

But You Were Too Busy to Listen

The good man brings good things out of the good stored up in his heart, and the evil man brings evil things out of the evil stored up in his heart. For out of the overflow of his heart his mouth speaks.

Luke 6:45

Jesus calls us from the worship, Of the vain world's golden store, From each idol that would keep us, Saying, "Christian, love me more."

"Jesus Calls Us o'er the Tumult"
Cecil Frances Alexander, 1852

The elect are the "whosoever-wills," and the non-elect are the "whosoever-won'ts."

—Henry Ward Beecher

Things Your Sunday School Teacher Told You...

As for God, his way is perfect; the word of the LORD is flawless. He is a shield for all who take refuge in him.

2 Samuel 22:31

If Joseph taught Sunday school his lesson would be: Don't fear the schemes of your enemies, God can use them for good.

For there is nothing hidden that will not be disclosed, and nothing concealed that will not be known or brought out into the open.

Luke 8:17

 42

But You Were Too Busy to Listen

In prayer it is better to have a heart without words, than words without a heart.

—John Bunyan

A hostile, egotistical attitude does not a hero make (from Proverbs 3:31–32).

To live with guns, security systems, and growling dogs is to live unprotected if you are living without God (from Psalm 20).

No one who puts his hand to the plow and looks back is fit for service in the kingdom of God.

Luke 9:62

He will give me grace and glory, And go with me, with me all the way.

> "Where he Leads Me"
> E.W. Blandy, 1890

The recurrence of the sweet and deep name, Father, unveils the secret of Christ's being.

> —Hugh Ross Mackintosh

Worship the LORD in the splendor of his holiness.

> 1 Chronicles 15:28

If Judah taught Sunday school his lesson would be: It's never too late to say "I'm sorry."

But You Were Too Busy to Listen

Ask and it will be given to you; seek and you will find; knock and the door will be opened to you.

Luke 11:9

The best throw of the dice is to throw them away.
—English Proverb

Wisdom is better than knowledge (from Proverbs 4:7).

Being called a sheep is the greatest compliment you can receive when God is your shepherd (from Psalm 23).

 45

Things Your Sunday School Teacher Told You...

Watch out! Be on your guard against all kinds of greed; a man's life does not consist in the abundance of his possessions.

Luke 12:15

O thou in whose presence my soul takes delight, On whom in affliction I call, My comfort by day and my song in the night, My hope, my salvation, my all.

"O Thou, in Whose Presence"
Frances R. Havergal, 1874

The best way to prepare for the coming of Christ is never to forget the presence of Christ.

—William Barclay

Things Your Sunday School Teacher Told You...

Be strong and courageous. Do not be afraid or discouraged.

1 Chronicles 22:13

If Jethro taught Sunday school his lesson would be: A good witness lives so that others can see God.

You also must be ready, because the Son of Man will come at an hour when you do not expect him.

Luke 12:40

The Lord gets his best soldiers out of the highlands of affliction.

—Charles Haddon Spurgeon

But You Were Too Busy to Listen

The road is always smooth when you do good deeds along the way (from Proverbs 4:11).

You can't have everything—God already owns it (from Psalm 24:1).

'Tis so sweet to trust in Jesus, Just to take him at his word; Just to rest upon his promise, Just to know, "Thus saith the Lord."

> "'Tis So Sweet to Trust in Jesus"
> Louisa M. R. Stead, 1882

It is always the case that when the Christian looks back, he is looking at the forgiveness of sins.

> —Karl Barth

Things Your Sunday School Teacher Told You...

Generations come and generations go, but the earth remains forever.

Ecclesiastes 1:4

If Moses taught Sunday school his lesson would be: God is able to use our weaknesses to his glory.

There is rejoicing in the presence of the angels of God over one sinner who repents.

Luke 15:10

He does not "believe" that does not live according to his "belief."

—Thomas Fuller

But You Were Too Busy to Listen

There are six things that the Lord hates:
Arrogance . . .
Lies (both black and white!) about yourself . . .
Lies (both black and white!) about others . . .
Spending time (and that means any time at all)
    plotting an evil scheme . . .
Looking forward to an evil scheme plotted by
    someone else . . .
And, of course, murder.

But wait, there's one more: Creating conflict among
your fellow Christians (from Proverbs 6:16–19).

The voice of the Lord doesn't need an amplifier to be heard or a synthesizer to fill us with wonder (from Psalm 29:3–5).

Whoever can be trusted with very little can also be trusted with much, and whoever is dishonest with very little will also be dishonest with much.

Luke 16:10

Faith is the victory, we know, That overcomes the world.

"Faith Is the Victory"
John H. Yates, 1891

But You Were Too Busy to Listen

Character is what you are in the dark.

—Dwight L. Moody

What has been will be again, what has been done will be done again; there is nothing new under the sun.

Ecclesiastes 1:9

If the children of Israel taught Sunday school their lesson would be: Complaining only makes the journey longer.

If your brother sins, rebuke him, and if he repents, forgive him.

Luke 17:3

Things Your Sunday School Teacher Told You...

Compassion will cure more sins than condemnation.
—Henry Ward Beecher

The advice of Godly parents is like a flashlight shining into the dark night when you can't find your way (from Proverbs 6:20–24).

God's anger is momentary but his mercy is eternal (from Psalm 30:5).

For God so loved the world that he gave his one and only Son, that whoever believes in him shall not perish but have eternal life.

John 3:16

But You Were Too Busy to Listen

For God did not send his Son into the world to condemn the world, but to save the world through him.

John 3:17

Punch and cookies are the snack foods of Bible memory champions.

I need thee ev'ry hour, Stay thou near by; Temptations lose their pow'r, When thou art nigh.

"I Need Thee Every Hour"
Annie S. Hawks, 1872

Beware lest clamor be taken for counsel.

—Erasmus

Things Your Sunday School Teacher Told You...

There is a time for everything, and a season for every activity under heaven.

Ecclesiastes 3:1

If the Levites taught Sunday school their lesson would be: We should worship the Lord because he alone is holy.

God is spirit, and his worshipers must worship in spirit and in truth.

John 4:24

The best interpreter of Christian doctrine is Christian work.

—George Augustus Selwyn

But You Were Too Busy to Listen

If you amble through life without any purpose, you will eventually run into someone who will choose one for you (from Proverbs 7:6–10).

Being envious of those who get ahead by hurting others is like admiring a weed that pushes the grain aside to grow: Both are tossed into the trash when the harvest comes (from Psalm 37).

Greater love has no one than this, that one lay down his life for his friends.

John 15:13

Things Your Sunday School Teacher Told You...

Never a trial that he is not there, Never a burden that he doth not bear, Never a sorrow that he doth not share, Moment by moment, I'm under his care.

"Moment by Moment"
Daniel W. Whittle, 1893

Let prayer be the key of the morning and the bolt of the evening.

—Matthew Henry

I know that everything God does will endure forever; nothing can be added to it and nothing taken from it.

Ecclesiastes 3:14

But You Were Too Busy to Listen

If Joshua taught Sunday school his lesson would be: A good leader knows when to be a willing follower.

The God who made the world and everything in it is the Lord of heaven and earth and does not live in temples built by hands.

Acts 17:24

Trust not to thy feeling, for whatever it be now; it will quickly be changed.

—Thomas a´ Kempis

But You Were Too Busy to Listen

If you always wear the armor of God's word, you will easily win every battle over temptation (from Proverbs 7:24–27).

If we help others when we are strong God will protect us when we are weak (from Psalm 41:1–3).

For it is not those who hear the law who are righteous in God's sight, but it is those who obey the law who will be declared righteous.

Romans 2:13

Things Your Sunday School Teacher Told You...

He's a Shepherd, kind and gracious, And his pastures are delicious; Constant love to me he shows, Yea, my very name he knows.

> "Jesus Makes My Heart Rejoice"
> Henriette Luise von Hayn, 1778

Of two evils choose neither.

> —Charles Haddon Spurgeon

God will bring to judgment both the righteous and the wicked, for there will be a time for every activity, a time for every deed.

> Ecclesiastes 3:17

But You Were Too Busy to Listen

If Ehud taught Sunday school his lesson would be: Never run up the white flag when your battle is against sin.

For the wages of sin is death, but the gift of God is eternal life in Christ Jesus our Lord.

Romans 6:23

Expect great things from God; attempt great things for God.

—William Carey

Stop, look, and listen are more than traffic rules: they are keys to wisdom (from Proverbs 8:9).

Things Your Sunday School Teacher Told You...

Y ou'll never be without a parent to guide you when God is your father (from Psalm 68:5).

P ut on the gospel armor, Each piece put on with prayer; Where duty calls, or danger, Be never wanting there.

"Stand Up, Stand Up for Jesus"
George Duffield, Jr., 1858

"I can forgive but I cannot forget" is only another way of saying "I cannot forgive."

—Henry Ward Beecher

But You Were Too Busy to Listen

Better a poor but wise youth than an old but foolish king who no longer knows how to take warning.

Ecclesiastes 4:13

If Deborah taught Sunday school her lesson would be: A good leader is respected not feared.

And we know that in all things God works for the good of those who love him, who have been called according to his purpose.

Romans 8:28

Things Your Sunday School Teacher Told You...

None can love freedom heartily but good men: the rest love license.

—John Milton

Only the good die old (from Proverbs 10:27).

The highest pedestal we can create for ourselves is looked down upon by God (from Psalm 75:6–7).

 66

But You Were Too Busy to Listen

Neither death nor life, neither angels nor demons, neither the present nor the future, nor any powers, neither height nor depth, nor anything else in all creation, will be able to separate us from the love of God that is in Christ Jesus our Lord.

Romans 8:38–39

Like a mighty army, Moves the church of God; Brothers we are treading, Where the saints have trod; We are not divided; All one body we, One in hope and doctrine, One in charity.

"Onward, Christian Soldiers"
Sabine Baring-Gould, 1864

A man there was, though some did count him mad, The more he cast away the more he had.

—John Bunyan

When times are good, be happy; but when times are bad, consider: God has made the one as well as the other.

Ecclesiastes 7:14

If Gideon taught Sunday school his lesson would be: We are all soldiers in the army of the Lord.

But You Were Too Busy to Listen

Do not conform any longer to the pattern of this world, but be transformed by the renewing of your mind. Then you will be able to test and approve what God's will is—his good, pleasing and perfect will.

Romans 12:2

Do not think of yourself more highly than you ought, but rather think of yourself with sober judgment, in accordance with the measure of faith God has given you.

Romans 12:3

We must know men to love them, but love God to know Him.

—Blaise Pascal

Life passes the evil man by because everything he does brings him closer to death (from Proverbs 11:19).

It's better to serve in God's house than to rule in a king's palace (from Psalm 84:10).

But You Were Too Busy to Listen

Run thou the race thro' God's good grace, Lift up thine eyes, and seek his face; Life with its way before us lies, Christ is the path, and Christ the prize.

"Fight the Good Fight"
John S.B. Monsell, 1863

All the beautiful sentiments in the world weigh less than a single lovely action.

—James Russell Lowell

Fear God and keep his commandments, for this is the whole duty of man.

Ecclesiastes 12:13

 71

Things Your Sunday School Teacher Told You...

If Gabriel taught Sunday school his lesson would be: Sound the trumpet and proclaim the good news of Jesus Christ to all the world.

If your enemy is hungry, feed him; if he is thirsty, give him something to drink. In doing this, you will heap burning coals on his head.

Romans 12:20

Do not be overcome by evil, but overcome evil with good.

Romans 12:21

Things Your Sunday School Teacher Told You...

Fashions may change but nothing will keep you alert in Sunday school like a starched white collar and stiff black shoes.

Our determination to imitate Christ should be such that we have no time for other matters.

—Erasmus

When you give to others you're really giving to yourself (from Proverbs 11:24–25).

Our praise is music to God's ears (from Psalm 92:1–3).

But You Were Too Busy to Listen

Give everyone what you owe him: If you owe taxes, pay taxes; if revenue, then revenue; if respect, then respect; if honor, then honor.

Romans 13:7

In seasons of distress and grief, My soul has often found relief, And oft escaped the tempter's snare, By thy return, sweet hour of prayer.

"Sweet Hour of Prayer"
William Walford, 1840

I know not where His islands lift, Their fronded palms in air: I only know I cannot drift, Beyond His love and care.

—John Greenleaf Whittier

Things Your Sunday School Teacher Told You...

Many waters cannot quench love; rivers cannot wash it away.

Song of Solomon 8:7

If Jephthah taught Sunday school his lesson would be: Don't make hasty promises to God without considering the consequences.

If Jephthah's daughter taught Sunday school her lesson would be: Don't let the foolishness of others discourage your commitment to the Lord.

But You Were Too Busy to Listen

For the kingdom of God is not a matter of eating and drinking, but of righteousness, peace and joy in the Holy Spirit, because anyone who serves Christ in this way is pleasing to God and approved by men.

Romans 14:17–18

As he that fears God fears nothing else, so he that sees God sees everything else.

—John Donne

An unkind deed never goes unnoticed (from Proverbs 11:31).

Things Your Sunday School Teacher Told You...

God's blessings are more abundant than our needs (from Psalm 107).

Do not deceive yourselves. If any one of you thinks he is wise by the standards of this age, he should become a "fool" so that he may become wise. For the wisdom of this world is foolishness in God's sight.

1 Corinthians 3:18–19

What a friend we have in Jesus, All our sins and griefs to bear!

"What a Friend We Have in Jesus"
Joseph Scriven, 1855

But You Were Too Busy to Listen

God is the only goal worthy of man's efforts; the fitting end of human existence is a loving union with God.

—Augustine

Though your sins are like scarlet, they shall be as white as snow; though they are red as crimson, they shall be like wool.

Isaiah 1:18

If Samson taught Sunday school his lesson would be: If you rely on physical strength then you may be blind to your spiritual weakness.

For the kingdom of God is not a matter of talk but of power.

1 Corinthians 4:20

There are but two kinds of men: the righteous who believe they are sinners, and the sinners who believe themselves righteous.

—Blaise Pascal

It is better to eat with dirty hands than to be too proud to work (from Proverbs 12:9).

Time spent in want is time spent in waste (from Psalm 112:10).

But You Were Too Busy to Listen

Do you not know that the wicked will not inherit the kingdom of God? Do not be deceived: Neither the sexually immoral nor idolaters nor adulterers nor male prostitutes nor homosexual offenders nor thieves nor the greedy nor drunkards nor slanderers nor swindlers will inherit the kingdom of God.

1 Corinthians 6:9–10

Are you weary, are you heavy hearted? Tell it to Jesus, Tell it to Jesus; Are you grieving over joys departed? Tell it to Jesus alone.

"Tell It to Jesus"
Jeremiah E. Rankin, 1888

Things Your Sunday School Teacher Told You...

We would have much peace if we would not busy ourselves with the sayings and doings of others.

—Thomas a´ Kempis

Stop trusting in man who has but a breath in his nostrils.

Isaiah 2:22

If Ruth taught Sunday school her lesson would be: Give your love without being asked for it.

If Naomi taught Sunday school her lesson would be: Give your love without asking for it in return.

But You Were Too Busy to Listen

If Boaz taught Sunday school his lesson would be:
Give your love without asking "What's in it for me?"

God is faithful; he will not let you be tempted
beyond what you can bear. But when you are
tempted, he will also provide a way out so that you
can stand up under it.

1 Corinthians 10:13

I have been many times to my knees by the
overwhelming conviction that I had nowhere else
to go.

—Abraham Lincoln

Success is spelled H–A–R–D W–O–R–K (from Proverbs 12:11).

The word of the Lord is a steady light along the path of life (from Psalm 119:105).

Lessons from The Love Chapter
The thirteenth chapter of 1 Corinthians

If I speak in the tongues of men and of angels, but have not love, I am only a resounding gong or a clanging cymbal.

Verse 1

But You Were Too Busy to Listen

If I have the gift of prophecy and can fathom all mysteries and all knowledge, and if I have a faith that can move mountains, but have not love, I am nothing.

Verse 2

If I give all I possess to the poor and surrender my body to the flames, but have not love, I gain nothing.

Verse 3

Love is patient, love is kind, it does not envy, it does not boast, it is not proud.

Verse 4

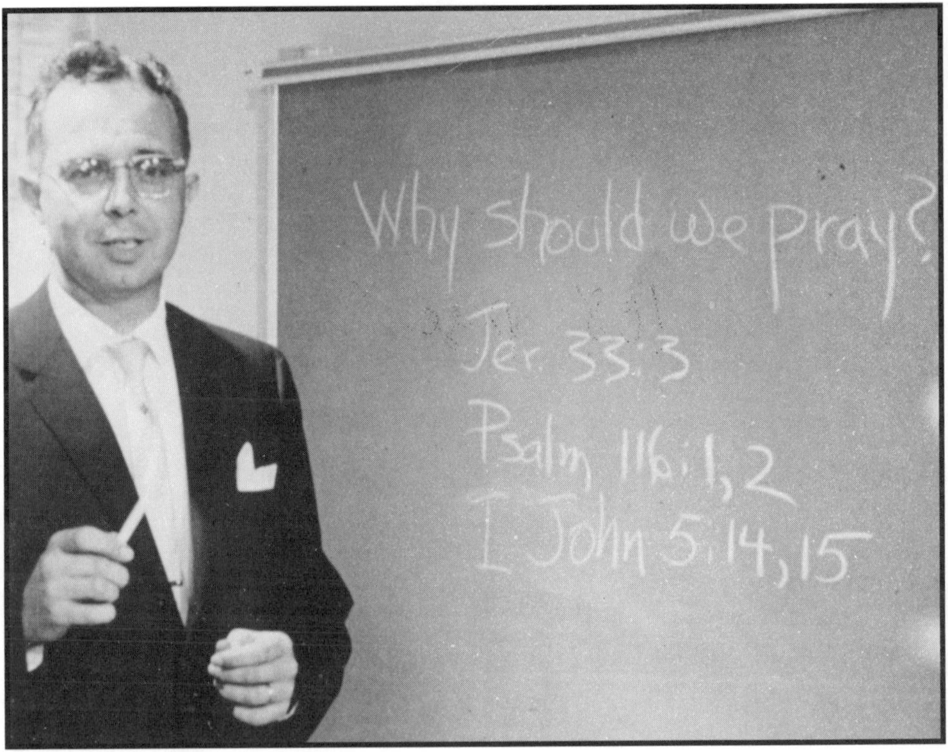
Why should we Pray?
Jer. 33:3
Psalm 116:1,2
I John 5:14,15

But You Were Too Busy to Listen

It is not rude, it is not self-seeking, it is not easily angered, it keeps no record of wrongs.

Verse 5

Love does not delight in evil but rejoices with the truth.

Verse 6

It always protects, always trusts, always hopes, always perseveres.

Verse 7

Love never fails. But where there are prophecies, they will cease; where there are tongues, they will be stilled; where there is knowledge, it will pass away.

Verse 8

For we know in part and we prophesy in part, but when perfection comes, the imperfect disappears.

Verses 9, 10

When I was a child, I talked like a child, I thought like a child, I reasoned like a child. When I became a man, I put childish ways behind me.

Verse 11

But You Were Too Busy to Listen

Now we see but a poor reflection; then we shall see face to face. Now I know in part; then I shall know fully, even as I am fully known.

Verse 12

And now these three remain: faith, hope and love. But the greatest of these is love.

Verse 13

Ready to go, ready to stay, Ready my place to fill; Ready for service, lowly or great, Ready to do his will.

"Ready"
A. C. Palmer, 1903

Things Your Sunday School Teacher Told You...

Rocking on the back two legs of your chair tells the world that your are doubly gifted with a superior sense of balance and an innate ability to press moon shaped holes in linoleum floors.

God is always listening.

—William Barclay

Woe to those who rise early in the morning to run after their drinks, who stay up late at night till they are inflamed with wine.

Isaiah 5:11

But You Were Too Busy to Listen

If Hannah taught Sunday school her lesson would be: A blessing returned to the Lord will be multiplied many times.

A man who hides behind the hypocrite is smaller than the hypocrite.

—William Edward Biederwolf

There is a fountain filled with blood, Drawn from Immanuel's veins; And sinners, plunged beneath that flood, Lose all their guilty stains.

"There Is a Fountain"
William Cowper, 1771

Things Your Sunday School Teacher Told You...

Wise words lighten a heavy heart (from Proverbs 12:25).

Going to church is the most fun you can have with another group of people (from Psalm 122:1).

For God is not a God of disorder but of peace.
1 Corinthians 14:33

When we walk with the Lord In the light of his Word What a glory he sheds on our way!
"When We Walk with the Lord"
John H. Sammis, 1887

But You Were Too Busy to Listen

Still waters are the deepest; the shallowest brooks brawl the most.

—Charles Haddon Spurgeon

Your priorities in life should be ordered by JOY: Jesus, Others, then Yourself.

Do not be misled: Bad company corrupts good character.

1 Corinthians 15:58

Woe to those who are wise in their own eyes and clever in their own sight.

Isaiah 5:21

Things Your Sunday School Teacher Told You...

If Eli taught Sunday school his lesson would be:
The sweet taste of public respect turns bitter when
you hide a private shame.

Your many sins are all forgiv'n, Oh! hear the voice
of Jesus; Go on your way in peace to heav'n, And
wear a crown with Jesus.

"The Great Physician"
William Hunter, 1859

A man may be damned for despairing to be saved.

—Jeremy Taylor

The Godly do not fear death; it is only the
beginning of eternal life (from Proverbs 12:28).

But You Were Too Busy to Listen

You will be as steady as a mountain if you trust in the Lord (from Psalm 125:1).

Always give yourselves fully to the work of the Lord, because you know that your labor in the Lord is not in vain.

1 Corinthians 15:58

And when thy face I see, My ransom'd soul shall be, Thro' all eternity, Something for thee.

"Something for Thee"
Sylvanus D. Phelps, 1864

The greatest of faults is to be conscious of none.
—Thomas Carlyle

Things Your Sunday School Teacher Told You...

Be on your guard; stand firm in the faith; be men of courage; be strong. Do everything in love.

1 Corinthians 16:13–14

In repentance and rest is your salvation, in quietness and trust is your strength.

Isaiah 30:15

Joy to the world! the Lord is come; Let earth receive her King; Let ev'ry heart prepare him room, And heav'n and nature sing, And heav'n and nature sing.

"Joy to the World! The Lord Is Come"
Isaac Watts, 1719

But You Were Too Busy to Listen

If Samuel taught Sunday school his lesson would be: If you take small responsibilities seriously then greater things will come your way.

We live by faith, not by sight.

2 Corinthians 5:7

The chains of habit are generally too small to be felt until they are too strong to be broken.

—Dwight L. Moody

The poor rich man envies the rich poor man (from Proverbs 13:7).

Things Your Sunday School Teacher Told You...

Each man should give what he has decided in his heart to give, not reluctantly or under compulsion, for God loves a cheerful giver.

2 Corinthians 9:7

If you've been sowing tears take heart because someday you'll harvest great joy (from Psalm 126:5).

And when we arrive at the haven of rest, We shall hear the glad words, "Come up hither, you blest, Here are regions of light, here are mansions of bliss." O who would not climb such a ladder as this?

"As Jacob with Travel"
Anonymous Folk Hymn

Things Your Sunday School Teacher Told You...

Clearly no one is justified before God by the law, because, "The righteous will live by faith."

Galatians 2:21

Earth hath no sorrow that heaven cannot heal.

—Sir Thomas More

For the Lord is a God of justice. Blessed are all who wait for him!

Isaiah 30:18

If your Sunday school teacher runs out the door with tears in her eyes its probably not because the class discussion blessed her.

But You Were Too Busy to Listen

The entire law is summed up in a single command: "Love your neighbor as yourself."

Galatians 4:24

If David taught Sunday school his lesson would be . . . accompanied by a full orchestra.

But if David came back the next Sunday he would settle down and his lesson would be: The first step toward repentance and forgiveness is to confess your sins.

Holiness is the architectural plan on which God buildeth up his living temple.

—Charles Haddon Spurgeon

Things Your Sunday School Teacher Told You...

But the fruit of the Spirit is love, joy, peace, patience, kindness, goodness, faithfulness, gentleness and self-control. Against such things there is no law.

Galatians 5:22–23

If you want to know what you will be like in the future, look at the people you spend time with now (from Proverbs 13:20).

The source of prosperity is respect for the Lord (from Psalm 128:1–2).

The family circle is the supreme conductor of Christianity.

—Henry Drummond

But You Were Too Busy to Listen

The acts of the sinful nature are obvious: sexual immorality, impurity and debauchery; idolatry and witchcraft; hatred, discord, jealousy, fits of rage, selfish ambition, dissensions, factions and envy; drunkenness, orgies, and the like. I warn you . . . that those who live like this will not inherit the kingdom of God.

Galatians 6:19–21

From him who loves me now so well, What pow'r my soul can sever? Shall life or death or earth or hell? No; I am his forever.

"I've Found a Friend, O Such a Friend"
James G. Small, 1863

Things Your Sunday School Teacher Told You...

Christianity is the good man's text; his life, the illustration.

—Joseph Thompson

The fruit of righteousness will be peace; the effect of righteousness will be quietness and confidence forever.

Isaiah 32:17

Do not be deceived: God cannot be mocked. A man reaps what he sows.

Galatians 6:7

If Jonathan taught Sunday school his lesson would be: Loyalty and courage often go hand in hand.

But You Were Too Busy to Listen

Conversion is a deep work—a heartwork. It goes throughout the man, throughout the mind, throughout the members, throughout the entire life.
—Joseph Alleine

He chose us in him before the creation of the world to be holy and blameless in his sight. In love he predestined us to be adopted as his sons through Jesus Christ, in accordance with his pleasure and will.

Ephesians 1:4–5

A good parent understands that love and discipline go hand in hand (from Proverbs 13:24).

Though our sins be abundant they cannot exceed the forgiveness of God (from Psalm 130:3–4).

He sends the sunshine and the rain, He sends the harvest's golden grain; Sunshine and rain, harvest of grain, He's my friend.

> "Jesus Is All the World to Me"
> Will L. Thompson, 1904

In him we have redemption through his blood, the forgiveness of sins, in accordance with the riches of God's grace.

> Ephesians 1:7

But You Were Too Busy to Listen

The grass withers and the flowers fall, but the word of our God stands forever.

Isaiah 40:8

Man should not consider his outward possessions as his own, but as common to all, so as to share them without hesitation when others are in need.

—Thomas Aquinas

But because of his great love for us, God, who is rich in mercy, made us alive with Christ even when we were dead in transgressions—it is by grace you have been saved.

Ephesians 2:4–5

If Abigail taught Sunday school her lesson would be: If you fall in love with someone who treats life like a carnival then your marriage may become a sideshow.

"Thou shalt not get found out" is not one of God's commandments; and no man can be saved by trying to keep it.

—Leonard Bacon

Be completely humble and gentle; be patient, bearing with one another in love.

Ephesians 4:2

But You Were Too Busy to Listen

Eat to live—the opposite is not very satisfying (from Proverbs 13:25).

Harmony is the melody of life (from Psalm 133).

Make every effort to keep the unity of the Spirit through the bond of peace.

Ephesians 4:3

All my hopes in thee abide, Thou my hope, and naught beside: Ever let my glory be, Only, only, only thee.

"Blessed Savior, Thee I Love"
George Duffield, Jr., 1851

Things Your Sunday School Teacher Told You...

It does not require great learning to be a Christian and be convinced of the truth of the Bible. It requires only an honest heart and a willingness to obey God.

—Albert Barnes

Do not let the sun go down while you are still angry.

Ephesians 4:26

Those who hope in the LORD will renew their strength. They will soar on wings like eagles; they will run and not grow weary, they will walk and not be faint.

Isaiah 40:31

But You Were Too Busy to Listen

Were the whole realm of nature mine, That were a present far too small; Love so amazing, so divine, Demands my soul, my life, my all.

> "When I Survey the Wondrous Cross"
> Isaac Watts, 1707

If Nathan taught Sunday school his lesson would be: Hold yourself to the same standards to which you hold others.

Life is like a Christmas pageant: Being a sheep is as important as being an angel.

But You Were Too Busy to Listen

He who has been stealing must steal no longer, but must work, doing something useful with his own hands, that he may have something to share with those in need.

Ephesians 4:28

Spend your time in nothing which you know must be repented of.

—Richard Baxter

There aren't any speed bumps on the road to destruction (from Proverbs 14:12).

Do not let any unwholesome talk come out of your mouths, but only what is helpful for building others up according to their needs, that it may benefit those who listen.

Ephesians 4:29

If God is love and God is eternal then so is his love (from Psalm 136:1).

No man of greater love can boast, Than for his friend to die: But for thy enemies thou was slain: What love with thine can vie!

"My Blessed Savior, Is Thy Love"
Joseph Stennett, 1697

But You Were Too Busy to Listen

Get rid of all bitterness, rage and anger, brawling and slander, along with every form of malice.

Ephesians 4:31

Be kind and compassionate to one another, forgiving each other, just as in Christ God forgave you.

Ephesians 4:32

Dislike what deserves it, but never hate, for that is of the nature of malice, which is applied to persons, not to things.

—William Penn

Things Your Sunday School Teacher Told You...

So do not fear, for I am with you; do not be dismayed, for I am your God. I will strengthen you and help you; I will uphold you with my righteous right hand.

Isaiah 41:10

If Solomon taught Sunday school his lesson would be: Even the wisest person will act foolish when he allows others to distract him from God.

Be very careful, then, how you live—not as unwise but as wise.

Ephesians 5:15

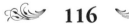 **116**

But You Were Too Busy to Listen

It is only the fear of God that can deliver us from the fear of man.

—John Witherspoon

Godliness is a lifetime adventure (from Proverbs 14:14).

If you've searched your heart and can find no faults then it's time to let God look for you (from Psalm 139:23–24).

Speak to one another with psalms, hymns and spiritual songs. Sing and make music in your heart to the Lord, always giving thanks to God the Father for everything, in the name of our Lord Jesus Christ.

Ephesians 5:19–20

There is never a day so dreary, There is never a night so long, But the soul that is trusting Jesus, Will somewhere find a song.

"Wonderful, Wonderful Jesus"
Anna B. Russell, 1921

One is never more on trial than in the moment of excessive good fortune.

—Lewis Wallace

But You Were Too Busy to Listen

Let him who boasts boast about this: that he understands and knows (the LORD) . . . who exercises kindness, justice and righteousness on earth.

Jeremiah 9:24

Put on the full armor of God so that you can take your stand against the devil's schemes.

Ephesians 6:11

Our struggle is not against flesh and blood, but against the rulers, against the authorities, against the powers of this dark world and against the spiritual forces of evil in the heavenly realms.

Ephesians 6:12

Things Your Sunday School Teacher Told You...

If Elijah taught Sunday school his lesson would be: God can silence our fears and discouragement with a whisper.

If Elisha taught Sunday school his lesson would be: It's difficult to fill the shoes of a great person unless God directs your steps.

A loving trust in the Author of the Bible is the best preparation for a wise and profitable study of the Bible itself.

—Henry Clay Trumbull

But You Were Too Busy to Listen

It is God who works in you to will and to act according to his good purpose.

Philippians 2:13

Do everything without complaining or arguing, so that you may become blameless and pure.

Philippians 2:14–15

Rejoice in the Lord always.

Philippians 4:4

Let your gentleness be evident to all.

Philippians 4:5

Things Your Sunday School Teacher Told You...

Do not be anxious about anything, but in everything, by prayer and petition, with thanksgiving, present your requests to God.

Philippians 4:6

Whatever is true, whatever is noble, whatever is right, whatever is pure, whatever is lovely, whatever is admirable—if anything is excellent or praiseworthy—think about such things.

Philippians 4:8

The poor are favored in God's eyes so make sure they are in yours (from Proverbs 14:31).

But You Were Too Busy to Listen

God's hand is a safe bridge over the pitfalls of life (from Psalm 142).

Yes, living, dying, let me bring, My strength, my solace from this spring, That he who lives to be my King, Once died to be my Savior.

"I Am Not Skilled to Understand"
Dora Greenwell, 1873

Sin may open bright as the morning, but it will end dark as night.

—Thomas DeWitt Talmage

Things Your Sunday School Teacher Told You...

A man's life is not his own; it is not for man to direct his steps.

Jeremiah 10:23

If Josiah taught Sunday school his lesson would be: True morality can only be legislated according to the laws of God.

The only morality that is clear in its source, pure in its precepts, and efficacious in its influence, is the morality of the gospel.

—John Sergeant

A kind word is worth more than a thousand arguments (from Proverbs 15:1).

Kingdoms come and kingdoms go but the kingdom of the Lord will last forever (from Psalm 145:13).

Set your minds on things above, not on earthly things.

Colossians 3:2

Whatever you do, work at it with all your heart, as working for the Lord, not for men.

Colossians 3:23

Devote yourselves to prayer, being watchful and thankful.

Colossians 4:2

But You Were Too Busy to Listen

Let your conversation be always full of grace, seasoned with salt, so that you may know how to answer everyone.

Colossians 4:6

He lives to bless me with his love, Glory, hallelujah! He lives to plead for me above, Glory, hallelujah!

"I Know that My Redeemer Lives"
Samuel Medley, 1775

Our bodies are but dust but they can bring praise to him that formed them.

—William Morley Punshon

Things Your Sunday School Teacher Told You...

If Ezra taught Sunday school his lesson would be: A great undertaking for God must be designed according to the blueprint of his word.

If Nehemiah taught Sunday school his lesson would be: A great undertaking for God must be designed according to the blueprint of his word . . . and built upon the altar of prayer.

It is God's will that you should be holy.

1 Thessalonians 4:3

For God did not call us to be impure, but to live a holy life.

1 Thessalonians 4:7

But You Were Too Busy to Listen

Make it your ambition to lead a quiet life, to mind your own business and to work with your hands . . . so that your daily life may win the respect of outsiders and so that you will not be dependent on anybody.

1 Thessalonians 4:11–12

The most important missionary journey a person can make is to walk next door.

If you're hungry for truth don't snack on moral junk food (from Proverbs 15:14).

Things Your Sunday School Teacher Told You...

Judge not the Lord by feeble sense, But trust him for his grace; Behind a frowning providence, He hides a smiling face.

> "God Moves in a Mysterious Way"
> William Cowper, 1774

We ask God to forgive us for our evil thoughts and evil temper, but rarely, if ever ask Him to forgive us for our sadness. Joy is a happy accident of the Christian life, an ornament and a luxury rather than a duty.

> —Robert William Dale

Be joyful always.

> 1 Thessalonians 5:16

But You Were Too Busy to Listen

Pray continually.

> 1 Thessalonians 5:17

Give thanks in all circumstances, for this is God's will for you in Christ Jesus.

> 1 Thessalonians 5:18

Do not put out the Spirit's fire.

> 1 Thessalonians 5:19

Do not treat prophecies with contempt.

> 1 Thessalonians 5:20

Test everything. Hold on to the good.

> 1 Thessalonians 5:21

Things Your Sunday School Teacher Told You...

Avoid every kind of evil.

1 Thessalonians 5:22

The LORD is good to those whose hope is in him, to the one who seeks him; it is good to wait quietly for the salvation of the LORD.

Lamentations 3:25–26

Everything looks brighter under a cheerful light (from Proverbs 15:15).

If Esther taught Sunday school her lesson would be: Physical beauty is only skin deep; putting others first makes one beautiful from the inside out.

But You Were Too Busy to Listen

If Job taught Sunday school his lesson would be: The enlightenment of the world becomes a murky darkness in the illumination of God's presence.

When the closing bell rings, the Sunday school lessons are just beginning.

The Lord is faithful, and he will strengthen and protect you from the evil one.

2 Thessalonians 3:3

Things Your Sunday School Teacher Told You...

There is no name so sweet on earth, No name so dear in heaven, As that before his wondrous birth, To Christ the Savior given.

"There Is No Name So Sweet"
George W. Bethune, 1861

All the duties of religion are eminently solemn and venerable in the eyes of children. But none will so strongly prove the sincerity of the parent as family devotions, particularly those in which petitions for the children occupy a distinguished place.

—Timothy Dwight

But You Were Too Busy to Listen

Have nothing to do with godless myths and old wives' tales; rather train yourself to be godly.

1 Timothy 4:7

Don't let anyone look down on you because you are young, but set an example for the believers in speech, in life, in love, in faith and in purity.

1 Timothy 4:12

Do not rebuke an older man harshly, but exhort him as if he were your father. Treat younger men as brothers, older women as mothers, and younger women as sisters, with absolute purity.

1 Timothy 5:1–2

Things Your Sunday School Teacher Told You...

We brought nothing into the world, and we can take nothing out of it.

1 Timothy 6:7

The love of money is a root of all kinds of evil.

1 Timothy 6:10

Who can speak and have it happen if the LORD has not decreed it?

Lamentations 3:37

The way to preserve the peace of the church is to preserve its purity.

—Matthew Henry

But You Were Too Busy to Listen

The prayers of the righteous never fall on deaf ears (from Proverbs 15:29).

If Isaiah taught Sunday school his lesson would be: Speaking a prophetic word from the Lord is like planting a seed—many seasons may pass before people appreciate its significance.

If Jeremiah taught Sunday school his lesson would be: Speaking a prophetic word from the Lord is like weeping for a lost cause—tears of grief may one day refresh the joy of God's people.

But You Were Too Busy to Listen

The confession of evil works is the first beginning of good works.

—Augustine

Avoid godless chatter, because those who indulge in it will become more and more ungodly.

2 Timothy 2:16

Don't have anything to do with foolish and stupid arguments, because you know they produce quarrels.

2 Timothy 2:23

If Mary taught Sunday school her lesson would be: Expect the unexpected from God.

Things Your Sunday School Teacher Told You...

If Joseph taught Sunday school his lesson would be: Social status has nothing to do with our position in the Kingdom of God.

If John the Baptist taught Sunday school his lesson would be: Even in the wilderness our voices must cry out the good news of salvation.

Warn a divisive person once, and then warn him a second time. After that, have nothing to do with him.

Titus 3:10

If the Pharisees taught Sunday school . . . start looking for another church across town.

But You Were Too Busy to Listen

Trusting him while life shall last, Trusting him till earth be past; Till within the jasper wall, Trusting Jesus, that is all.

"Trusting Jesus"
Edgar Page Stites, 1876

Doctrine is the framework of life—the skeleton of truth, to be clothed and rounded out by the living grace of a holy life.

—Adoniram Judson Gordon

You can't please God by pleasing man, but you can please man by pleasing God (from Proverbs 16:7).

Things Your Sunday School Teacher Told You...

The word of God is living and active. Sharper than any double-edged sword, it penetrates even to dividing soul and spirit, joints and marrow; it judges the thoughts and attitudes of the heart.

Hebrews 4:12

Nothing in all creation is hidden from God's sight. Everything is uncovered and laid bare before the eyes of him to whom we must give account.

Hebrews 4:13

If we deliberately keep on sinning after we have received the knowledge of the truth, no sacrifice for sins is left.

Hebrews 10:26

But You Were Too Busy to Listen

Faith is being sure of what we hope for and certain of what we do not see.

Hebrews 11:1

Do not make light of the Lord's discipline, and do not lose heart when he rebukes you, because the Lord disciplines those he loves and he punishes everyone he accepts as a son.

Hebrews 12:5–6

If the thief on the cross taught Sunday school his lesson would be: It's never too late to give your heart to Jesus.

Things Your Sunday School Teacher Told You...

I have a home prepared for me, Since I have been redeemed, Where I shall dwell eternally, Since I have been redeemed.

"Since I Have Been Redeemed"
Edwin O. Excell, 1884

We can do more good by being good than in any other way.

—Rowland Hill

Fairness: God's first principle for success in business (from Proverbs 16:11).

But You Were Too Busy to Listen

If the boy with the loaves and fishes taught Sunday school his lesson would be: God takes our offering and multiplies it to his glory and our needs.

Consider it pure joy . . . whenever you face trials of many kinds, because you know that the testing of your faith develops perseverance.

James 1:2–3

Blessed is the man who perseveres under trial, because when he has stood the test, he will receive the crown of life that God has promised to those who love him.

James 1:12

When tempted, no one should say, "God tempted me." For God cannot be tempted by evil, nor does he tempt anyone.

James 1:13

Every good and perfect gift is from above, coming down from the Father of the heavenly lights, who does not change like shifting shadows.

James 1:17

If anyone considers himself religious and yet does not keep a tight rein on his tongue, he deceives himself and his religion is worthless.

James 1:26

But You Were Too Busy to Listen

For where you have envy and selfish ambition, there you find disorder and every evil practice.

James 3:16

Peacemakers who sow in peace raise a harvest of righteousness.

James 3:18

Anyone who speaks against his brother or judges him, speaks against the law and judges it.

James 4:11

Anyone . . . who knows the good he ought to do and doesn't do it, sins.

James 4:17

Confess your sins to each other and pray for each other so that you may be healed. The prayer of a righteous man is powerful and effective.

James 5:16

Christ the Lord is ris'n today, Alleleluia! Sons of men and angels say, Alleleluia! Raise your joys and triumphs high, Alleluia! Sing, ye heav'ns, and earth, reply, Alleluia!

"Christ the Lord Is Risen Today"
Charles Wesley, 1739

But You Were Too Busy to Listen

If the Disciples taught Sunday school their lessons would be:

Simon Peter—Even the best of Christians falter but Jesus will guide their steps back to him.

James (son of Zebedee)—To die for Jesus is to live in his glory forever.

John—To be a "Son of Thunder" you must first love the Son of God.

Andrew—God wants us all to be fishers of men.

Philip—Jesus is Lord.

Bartholomew—God gives honest answers to honest questions.

Matthew—The only investment that will profit your soul is the one you make in the cross.

Things Your Sunday School Teacher Told You...

Thomas—When we give our doubts to Christ he transforms them into faith.

James (son of Alphaeus)—Just because you stand in the background doesn't mean that God hasn't chosen you for the front lines.

Thaddaeus—Belief should not always be based on understanding.

Simon the Zealot—Christians are patriots of the Kingdom of God.

I know I shall see in his beauty, The King in whose law I delight; Who lovingly guardeth my footsteps, And giveth me songs in the night.

"Redeemed, How I Love to Proclaim It"
Fanny J. Crosby, 1882

Things Your Sunday School Teacher Told You...

The person who has control over self is more powerful than the one who has control over many (from Proverbs 16:32).

O there's sunshine, blessed sunshine, When the peaceful, happy moments roll; When Jesus shows his smiling face, There is sunshine in my soul.

"Sunshine in My Soul"
Eliza E. Hewitt, 1887

As obedient children, do not conform to the evil desires you had when you lived in ignorance.

1 Peter 1:14

But You Were Too Busy to Listen

Live such good lives among the pagans that, though they accuse you of doing wrong, they may see your good deeds and glorify God on the day he visits us.

1 Peter 2:12

Each one should use whatever gift he has received to serve others, faithfully administering God's grace in its various forms.

1 Peter 4:10

Cast all your anxiety on him because he cares for you.

1 Peter 5:7

Be self-controlled and alert. Your enemy the devil prowls around like a roaring lion looking for someone to devour.

1 Peter 5:8

If Mary and Martha taught Sunday school their lesson would be: Men and women are truly equal in the eyes of the Lord.

You must understand that no prophecy of Scripture came about by the prophet's own interpretation. For prophecy never had its origin in the will of man, but men spoke from God as they were carried along by the Holy Spirit.

2 Peter 1:20–21

But You Were Too Busy to Listen

Do not forget this one thing . . . With the Lord a day is like a thousand years, and a thousand years are like a day.

2 Peter 3:8

A comfortable old age is the reward of a well-spent youth; instead of its introducing dismal and melancholy prospects of decay, it should give us hopes of eternal youth in a better world.

—Ray Palmer

If Paul taught Sunday school his lesson would be: If sin has made you blind, God's holiness will make you see.

Things Your Sunday School Teacher Told You...

The less you talk the more people think you have to say (from Proverbs 17:2–28).

His perfect salvation, his wonderful love, I'll shout with the millions on high.

> "He Hideth My Soul"
> Fanny J. Crosby, 1890

There is no leveler like Christianity, but it levels by lifting all who receive it to the lofty table-land of a true character and of undying hope both for this world and the next.

> —Jonathan Edwards

But You Were Too Busy to Listen

The shelter of a rich man is paper thin (from Proverbs 18:11).

His Word will stand forever, ever; His truth—it shall be My shield and buckler, So I'm not afraid.

"I Will Not Be Afraid"
Anonymous

If we claim to be without sin, we deceive ourselves and the truth is not in us.

1 John 1:8

If we confess our sins, he is faithful and just and will forgive us our sins and purify us from all unrighteousness.

1 John 1:9

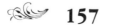

Anyone who claims to be in the light but hates his brother is still in the darkness.

1 John 2:9

The world and its desires pass away, but the man who does the will of God lives forever.

1 John 2:17

Love (not) with words or tongue but with actions and in truth.

1 John 3:18

But You Were Too Busy to Listen

Do not believe every spirit, but test the spirits to see whether they are from God, because many false prophets have gone out into the world.

1 John 4:1

There is no fear in love. But perfect love drives out fear, because fear has to do with punishment. The man who fears is not made perfect in love.

1 John 4:18

Rejoice, the Lord is King: Your Lord and King adore!

"Rejoice, the Lord Is King"
Charles Wesley, 1744

Things Your Sunday School Teacher Told You...

In his life, Christ is an example, showing us how to live; in his death, he is a sacrifice, satisfying for our sins; in his resurrection, a conqueror; in his ascension, a king; in his intercession, a high priest.
—Martin Luther

In the last times there will be scoffers who will follow their own ungodly desires. These are the men who divide you, who follow mere natural instincts and do not have the Spirit.

Jude 18–19

Your family tree will bear good fruit when it is rooted in honesty (from Proverbs 20:7).

But You Were Too Busy to Listen

Come to this fountain so rich and sweet, Cast thy poor soul at the Savior's feet; Plunge in today, and be made complete; Glory to his name.

"Down at the Cross"
Elisha A. Hoffman, 1878

The fastest ways to reveal your secrets are by telephone, telegraph, and tell-a-gossip (from Proverbs 20:19).

Praise in the common things of life, Its goings out and in; Praise in each duty and each deed, However small and mean.

"Fill Thou My Life, O Lord My God"
Horatius Bonar, 1866

The Christian life is not merely knowing or hearing, but doing the will of Christ.

Frederick William Robertson

The steps of a good man are ordered by the Lord (from Proverbs 20:24).

How sweet the name of Jesus sounds, In a believer's ear! It soothes sorrows, heals his wounds, And drives away his fear.

"How Sweet the Name of Jesus Sounds"
John Newton, 1779

But You Were Too Busy to Listen

It is more prestigious to have gold in the bank than to have a gold covered credit card (from Proverbs 21:20).

In his boundless love and mercy, He the ransom freely gave.

"I Will Sing of My Redeemer"
Philip P. Bliss, 1876

A closed mouth attracts wise thoughts; an open mouth only flies (from Proverbs 21:23).

But You Were Too Busy to Listen

Take the name of Jesus ever, As a shield from ev'ry snare; When temptations round you gather, Breathe that holy name in pray'r.

> "Take the Name of Jesus with You"
> Lydia Baxter, 1870

God places more value on our motives than our money (from Proverbs 22:2).

Was e'er a gift like the Savior given? No, not one! No, not one! Will he refuse us a home in heaven? No, not one! No, not one!

> "No, Not One"
> Johnson Oatman, Jr., 1895

Things Your Sunday School Teacher Told You...

Strength is measured by a wise heart, not a strong arm (from Proverbs 24:5).

All for Jesus, all for Jesus, This the church's song must be, Till, at last, we then are gathered, One in love and one in thee.

> "All for Jesus, All for Jesus"
> William J. Sparrow Simpson, 1887

If you sleep too much, poverty will soon be your pillow (from Proverbs 24:32–34).

But You Were Too Busy to Listen

When we all get to heaven, What a day of rejoicing that will be! When we all see Jesus, We'll sing and shout the victory.

"When We All Get to Heaven"
Eliza E. Hewitt, 1898

A lying tongue is a dangerous weapon that should never be loaded (from Proverbs 25:18).

There's a land that is fairer than day, And by faith we can see it afar; For the Father waits over the way, To prepare us a dwelling place there.

"There's a Land That Is Fairer than Day"
Sanford F. Bennett, 1868

Things Your Sunday School Teacher Told You...

It's better to limp all the way to heaven than to not get there at all.

—William A. "Billy" Sunday

The grace of the Lord Jesus be with God's people. Amen.

Revelation 22:21

If you've decided you're too old for Sunday school then you're not as mature as you think.

A portrait of the author/
editor as a young man.

Dear Reader,

If your Sunday school teacher taught you something that you didn't find in this book, please write it down with your name and address (you may include your teacher's name as well if you like) and mail it to **500 Things, P.O. Box 150009, Nashville, TN 37215**. We would welcome the privilege of including it in a future volume. Thanks!

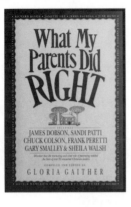

Compiled by Gloria Gaither, **What My Parents Did Right** is an inspiring and encouraging book about the importance of family and the positive role parents can play in their children's lives.

Over 50 renowned Christians—each one a leader in ministry, business, politics, or the arts—share how their own lives have been transformed by loving, dedicated parents.

Contributors include Dr. James Dobson, Tony Campolo, Janette Oke, Frank Peretti, Charles Colson, Sandi Patti and many, many more.

Clothbound *$17.99*

Based on the best-selling book, the **What My Parents Did Right Family Album Video** will introduce you—through dramatic reenactments of childhood memories, intimate conversations, and rare historical footage—to some of today's most influential Christian leaders, and the selfless people who molded their character.

Volume I features Gloria Gaither, Bill Gaither, Dr. Ben Carson, Charles Colson, Dr. James Dobson, Sheila Walsh, and Sandi Patti.

Volume II features Danae Dobson, Joni Eareckson-Tada, Carman, Kim Hill, Mark Lowry, Twila Paris, and Michael W. Smith.

60 minute VHS Video .... *$19.99 each*

In **September Song** Dr. Leslie Moser, Professor of the Psychology of Aging at Baylor University, offers tremendous insight into the aging process. Dr. Moser addresses the role advancing age plays in a person's mental, physical, and spiritual development.

Clothbound *$12.99*

For more than a decade, Missy Tate has been ministering to senior adults throughout the United States in churches, nursing homes, and retirement centers. Her beautiful soprano voice and tender compassion have touched lives clouded by loneliness, pain, and worry.

Gifts of Assurance includes a large print book devoted to God's promises for older Christians and a cassette tape containing 12 beautifully orchestrated hymns of the faith.

Christmas Never Ages presents the hope of the Christmas message to senior citizens who might otherwise find the holiday season a time of loneliness and despair. This package includes a large print book expressing the joy of Christmas and 12 beautifully orchestrated hymns of the season.

Cassette and Booklet .... *$14.99 each*

These and other Star Song Publishing Group products are available at your local Christian bookstore or through
Star Song•P.O. Box 150009•Nashville•TN•37215
(615)269-0196

COLOPHON

Cover Design by Karen Philpott
of Rogers and Brandon, Nashville, Tennessee

Interior Design and Layout by David R. West, Jr.

Substantive Editing by Jeanie Price

Copy Editing by Amanda Sauer

Page Composition was done using Aldus PageMaker

Printed and Bound by Versa Press, Peoria, Illinois